BAPTISM

An Important Step in Your Life with Christ

Jim Spruce

BEACON HILL PRESS
OF KANSAS CITY

ISBN 978-0-8341-2938-2

Printed in the
United States of America

Cover Design: Keith Alexander
Interior Design: Sharon Page

Library of Congress Cataloging-in-Publication Data

Spruce, James R.
  Baptism : an important step in your life with Christ / Jim Spruce.
    pages cm
  Includes bibliographical references.
  ISBN 978-0-8341-2938-2 (pbk.)
  1. Baptism. I. Title.
  BV811.3.S69 2013
  234'.161—dc23

                                                    2012045082

10 9 8 7 6 5 4 3 2 1

To
my mother, Irene,
my sister, Sara,
and our grandchildren,
Elisabeth, Olivia, Jacks, Cecy,
C. J., Liam, and Khaya

Contents

Preface and Acknowledgments

Baptism is considered a sacrament by nearly all Wesleyan churches. Despite the differences of opinion that surround this subject, it is vital to begin conversing about it. Understanding the sacrament of baptism and why Christians should pursue it are essential parts of the discussion.

Although this book is not intended to be a comprehensive study, it is designed to be a helpful guide. In it you'll find consideration given to issues such as choosing between infant baptism and infant dedication. Parents, in this case, are advised to approach this decision thoughtfully, keeping in mind that no matter which option they choose, presenting their baby or child to the Lord is more important than doing nothing at all. Other matters of practice and significance surrounding baptism are handled in a similar fashion.

I am grateful to Bonnie Perry and Richard Buckner at Nazarene Publishing House. I am in debt to my wife, Karen, for her insight and long-suffering spirit. Our children, Cynthia, Steven, and Sharolyn, now adults, were at home when I was a father and pastor, and each in his or her special way contributed more than he or she ever knew to my life. Darrin Grinder, my son-in-law, and pastors John Connett, Larry Lacher, and David Young offered invaluable criticism.

My sister, Sara, and I grew up in Nazarene parsonages and were baptized by our dad. We know we personally benefited from godly parents who embodied the Spirit of Christ.

one

PILGRIMAGE

The Journey That Got You Here

Mackie* was among the adults and children who stood at the altar rail that Sunday. They were new candidates for baptism, and an atmosphere of expectation and gratitude filled the church. The pastor read the formal and solemn words from the church's ritual on the sacrament of baptism.

This was a joyous event, but it was also sobering because Mackie was there. When Jesus died for Mackie, he died for a lot of stuff. Some of us knew most of the story, a story of heartbreak, sin, and loss. Even so, Mackie took his place by the altar. No doubt he felt as different as he looked, for he was the only single guy in a company of married couples and children. But he was there nonetheless, a testimony to God's grace!

Other than infants and very young children, candidates who have reached an age of moral responsibility come to the water after they have first come to God seeking forgiveness for their sins.

---

*Not his real name.

Sin separates us from God, the gift of salvation restores us to his favor, and the sacrament of baptism affirms our public testimony to God, who sought us before we sought him. All of us who are candidates for baptism—the not so bad and the really bad—have our own pilgrimages, our own journeys, through which we discovered our need for God. Truly none of us is so good that we are exempt from baptism or so bad that we are unfit for it.

A sacrament is "a sacred, religious act symbolizing a spiritual reality, especially one instituted or recognized by Jesus Christ."[1] Baptism is a participatory sacrament in which a candidate shares in the sacred and now ancient ritual of showing loyalty to God's Son. This is a holy event, a moment to tell everyone that we are aligning ourselves with the Lord who forgave our sins and that we no longer live for ourselves.

When we say that baptism is a sacrament, we identify its significance historically and biblically. Since the time of Jesus, both baptism and the Lord's Supper (Communion) were sacraments that were offered in the Christian church. While Christian churches have differed over the sacraments for centuries, nearly all continue to employ baptism and Communion as necessary features of public worship. Participating in the sacraments is not a light matter: "It is no meaningless ritual we perform when we observe His ordinances, no piece of [religious] mumbo-jumbo; sacramental practice is full of Gospel truth, and is intended for our enrichment."[2]

The Bible aids our understanding because it links baptism with repentance and Christ's death and resurrection and with all three persons of the Trinity. On the day of Pentecost, Peter boldly stated, "Repent and be baptized, every one of you, in the name of Jesus Christ for the forgiveness of your sins. And you will receive the gift of the Holy Spirit" (Acts 2:38). Baptism declares to everyone that we have "received Christ as Savior and Lord, having repented and believed the gospel."[3] Repentance means that we acknowledge and confess our personal sins before God, seek his forgiveness, and turn from our sins to God.

Scripture affirms the Trinity in the ritual of baptism. Matthew records the last words of Jesus in the Great Commission: "Therefore go and make disciples of all nations, baptizing them in the name of the Father and of the Son and of the Holy Spirit" (28:19). One author states that baptism is the "application of water in the name of the Father, Son and Holy [Spirit], as an outward sign of an inward work of grace."[4] To be baptized in the name of the Father, Son, and Holy Spirit is to acknowledge the presence and unique ministry of each person of the Trinity in our lives for the rest of our lives.

Scripture identifies Christ's death and resurrection with baptism. The apostle Paul's letter to the Romans states, "Therefore we have been buried with Him through baptism into death, so that as Christ was raised from the dead through the glory of the Father, so we too might walk in newness of life" (6:4, NASB). Michael Lodahl offers "that baptism is a reenactment of Jesus' own death and resurrection, whereby the believer is united with Christ. In baptism, then, the believer identifies with the story of Jesus' death and resurrection as his or her radically new way of thinking and being."[5]

The story that brings anyone to baptism is enlightened not only by Scripture but also by personal experience. The life lessons we learn not only are academic but often include an unwanted mosaic of misery as well. Yet pain is "God's megaphone," as C. S. Lewis reminded us.[6]

When the church of my childhood was remodeled in the mid-1950s, a baptismal tank was installed. I was twelve, a new Christian, and eager to be baptized. (Actually, I was probably more interested in seeing what it would be like to get into a full tank of water and then swim my way out after being baptized.) My dad was the pastor, so I figured I at least had a chance.

But my dad had several compelling questions to ask me. Among other things he asked if I understood what God in Christ did to forgive sins and if my sins were truly forgiven. He asked if I loved God more than myself. He asked if I really wanted to be known publicly as a Christian.

Fortunately I lived in a more innocent time and was still too young and sheltered to have gone very far into sin. I am not sure I completely grasped the weight of his searching queries at my young age. However, such questions are still challenging and relevant for baptismal candidates today and should help shape important conversations with candidates in classes or small groups or between candidates and their mentors or pastors.

Consider two issues that usually come to light as we reflect on our journey in the light of these kinds of telling questions:

First, the difference between God and us is that he is sovereign (without limits to his power) and we are not. A person's grasp of this fact may come earlier or later depending on his or her age, spiritual sensitivity, emotional maturity, length and type of religious memory, and so on.

God's sovereignty places him on a completely different plane of existence than ours. He rules. He determines. He is eternal. He is the "wholly other" or "that which is quite beyond the sphere of the usual, . . . filling the mind with . . . astonishment."[7] In contrast, we may jog in the park, work feverishly at our jobs, and even go on a multitude of business trips all over the world. We may even be prominent leaders in the church and community, but none of these things is enough to qualify us for baptism or get us into heaven.

As a candidate for baptism, a person must come to grips with the knowledge that he or she is nowhere close to being what God is like—One who is so magnificent, so incredible, and so beyond description. But when a person accepts God for who he is, then he or she can accept and finally trust his sovereignty. It is wonderful to have a sovereign God when we know that we ourselves are not sovereign. God's sovereignty is designed to destabilize a person's self-sovereignty, giving him or her a humble spirit in preparation for baptism.

Second, God's redeeming love sought us out to forgive our sins and make us his beloved children before we were aware of it. This is the singular and ultimate favor of God in which he bestows mercy and grace through the gift of his Son. The ritual of baptism reminds us that the God of Scripture paid an enormous price to offer his own Son in baptism and death so that we, as Lodahl said, might experience a "radically new way of thinking and being."[8]

One time a little boy, only five years old, stole a pocket watch from his grandpa's attic. Even at his young age he knew it was wrong. He knew it was wrong because he had to hide the watch everywhere he went: first in his pocket; then in a dresser drawer, under the linens; and later under the car seat when his family drove home from his grandpa's house. He couldn't talk about it and couldn't show it to anyone. It wasn't his to enjoy. But the truth came out. You cannot hide a thick watch from your mom forever. The little boy had to admit the watch was not given to him. Many years later, all this memory returned to him at the time of his conversion, when he repented and sought God's forgiveness. And at his baptism he realized this painful experience was now behind him.[9] The pilgrimage of the baptized in Christ, with its sometimes painful reminders, does indeed usher in a "new way of thinking and being"[10] in relationship to Christ.

The journey that brings us to the water for baptism may have been "thro' many dangers, toils and snares,"[11] but we have a friend who went before us. The story that got us to baptism did not really begin with us—it began in Jesus Christ!

two
TRANSFORMATION
A New Identity in Christ

Most of us have several ways people can identify us. Our names and addresses are just a couple. We also have driver's licenses and passports with lengthy numbers and unflattering photos. Credit scores, social security numbers, and birth certificates also shed light on who we are. All these identifications and many more say something significant about us. They provide information to institutions and governing agencies that have an interest in us—that want to know our identity. But beyond all the officials, bureaus, and agencies, God has the greatest interest in who we really are.

As the One who is most interested in our identity, God said that if we are baptized into his Son, Jesus Christ, we are also baptized into the very *death* of Christ (Rom. 6:3). Baptism symbolically affirms that we have accepted all that the death of Christ meant to our Lord into our own being and purpose for living. It is transformational, completely reordering the way we think, live, and act. At baptism we publicly agree to live like Jesus: without the practice of sin. This decision is not made through our own strength; rather, it is rooted in the strength of Christ, in whom baptism confirms for us a new identity.

William Greathouse affirmed, "When Christ died, he died to sin, forever. His death completely and finally severed him from contact with sin. Just so, our baptism is a sign and seal of our death to sin, *our* severance from sin. 'To be baptized into Christ's shameful death is to quit the life of sin. The divisive competition for honor is exposed and laid to rest by the cross.'"[1] Baptism is thus public notice and stunning proof that we are serious enough with God to cut the last remaining tie to our engagement with the life of sin.

Our identity is no longer in whatever sinful or self-centered intention we might have employed in the old days of sin before our salvation. Our new identity is in Jesus Christ. Frankly, water baptism is a great introduction and precursor to another baptism, the baptism with the Holy Spirit.

Baptism is a way of nailing down a person's determination to live like Jesus. There is just no other way about it—once saved, a Christ-follower has made the choice to walk in all the spiritual light God provides or risk abandoning covenants made and stalling out. Accepting the sacrament of baptism is like driving a stake in the ground and saying, "This is where I will show the commitment I have made; I will not be deterred."

Martin Luther rested on such an assurance during a troublesome period in his life. As a young priest he had serious theological differences with the Catholic Church in the 1500s and ultimately separated from it. Though later credited with initiating a spiritual reformation in Germany and with establishing the Lutheran Church, Luther suffered considerable persecution. He "often became so despondent that he could virtually sense Satan slithering to his side and sorely tempting him to doubt his salvation. In such times, he could cause the devil to slink away by declaring emphatically, 'I am baptized!'"[2] May it be so with us.

In the light of the awesome value some Christians place on baptism, it is unfortunate that many Christ-followers today underestimate the significance of this sacrament. But that was not the case in Jesus' day. The Lord's cousin John the Baptist and the Lord's disciples baptized repenters. Immediately after Pentecost thousands were baptized. Apparently the early church of the New Testament considered baptism an expectation of all followers of Christ, so that "there were no unbaptized Christians, except for [those] who were still preparing for church membership."[3] So it only seemed natural to the followers of Christ that they would be baptized.

Remarkably, both John and Jesus symbolize the reality that God is present and can forgive sins and acknowledge sins forgiven in places other than the temple—a radical idea in first-century Judaism. In the New Testament, baptism was identification with a kingdom movement, not simply a decision of human will.

Would Jesus, the sinless Son of God and second person of the Trinity, offer himself as a candidate for baptism? He did indeed, and at that moment Christ revealed two essential aspects of his character. First, Jesus proved his humility and commitment to a sinless life of loyalty to his heavenly Father. Second, our Lord evidenced his passion to identify with people hopelessly lost in sin so that they might identify with all that his baptism meant to him.

We know our story, the journey that brings us to baptism. But this was Jesus' story, that he came to baptism with a fervent intent to live a sinless life, though the opportunity to sin surrounded him, just as it does any other human. "For we do not have a high priest who is unable to empathize with our weaknesses, but we have one who has been tempted in every way, just as we are—yet he did not sin" (Heb. 4:15). If anything, Jesus' submission to the ritual of baptism identified his humanity and thereby linked him with our humanity. How true it is that "if our own baptism involves an identification with Jesus, it is noteworthy that his baptism, in obedience to the will of God, is an act of identification with us as sinners."[4]

Thus at the initiation of his public ministry Jesus demonstrated an attitude toward his Father that he hoped we would notice and copy. Baptism in the Jordan River did not save Jesus in a spiritual sense any more than water baptism saves us from our sins. Baptism is the indication of our salvation, not the cause of it. But baptism certainly *revealed* Jesus' willingness to obey God all the way to the cross.

What, then, does this new identity in Christ mean?

First, our new identity in Christ at last reveals who we were intended to be all along—God's beloved children. Prior to our salvation, our former self—who we were while in sin—was cloaked in all the drab consequences of our alienation from God. We were wandering pilgrims, stumbling along in blind indifference to the true self God wanted us to become. Paul wrote the Ephesians, "Remember that . . . you were separate from Christ . . . without hope and without God in the world" (2:12).

Then something happened. Like Jesus' incomparable parable of the prodigal son, our eyes were opened and what we saw astonished us. We saw what we had become away from the Father in contrast to what we could be right alongside him. We realized that what we had gained or done through our own frail efforts was nothing compared to the love and status that would be ours to enjoy once we were reunited at home with our Father.

The apostle Paul captured it best: "But God demonstrates his own love for us in this: While we were still sinners, Christ died for us" (Rom. 5:8). Stuart Townend said it in a hymn:

> I will not boast in anything,
> No gifts, no power, no wisdom;
> But I will boast in Jesus Christ,
> His death and resurrection.
>
> Why should I gain from His reward?
> I cannot give an answer,
> But this I know with all my heart,
> His wounds have paid my ransom.[5]

Jesus' baptism initiated the mission that would take him to the cross and thus his ultimate ministry to us while we were in sin, as well as his unimaginable plan for us. Only God knows all we are intended to be, and as soon as sin is forgiven and the remnants of the old life are washed away, the new and amended version will begin to emerge. *That* is what identity in Christ confirms and what baptism celebrates.

Second, our new identity in Christ is symbolized by the invisible mark of water baptism. John Wesley, instrumental in founding Methodism and promoter of the English Reformation in the 1700s, saw water baptism as the New Testament counterpart to the Old Testament custom of circumcision: "As circumcision was then the way of entering into this covenant, so baptism is now."[6]

God identifies his people through baptism; it is simply his way of saying (in a fashion less painful than that of the old covenant), "These are my people; I have chosen to identify them in this manner." In his sermon "A Treatise on Baptism," Wesley clarifies the importance of baptism. It is "to remain always in [Christ's] Church. . . . It is the initiatory sacrament, which enters us into covenant with God. It was instituted by Christ . . . [as a] means of grace, perpetually obligatory on all Christians. . . . And it was instituted in the room of [or in place of] circumcision."[7]

Baptism is not a cheap event. It is not a means to gain religious popularity. The price that Jesus paid for us to be baptized resulted in his being marked, scandalized, by the cross in such a way as to make a strong person think twice about the price of this sacrament. The physical marks Christ bore as a result of his baptism came from the cross just as Isaiah rightly prophesied: "But he was pierced for our transgressions, he was crushed for our iniquities" (53:5). Baptism was the initial act that took our Lord to the cross.

How did the Father feel, what did the Father think, when his Son suffered such reproach for choosing this sacrament? Townend's haunting lyrics speak again:

> *How deep the Father's love for us,*
> *How vast beyond all measure,*
> *That He should give His only Son*
> *To make a wretch His treasure.*
>
> *How great the pain of searing loss,*
> *The Father turns His face away,*
> *As wounds which mar the Chosen One*
> *Bring many sons to glory.*[8]

No identifiable marks or scars from water baptism? Consider that countless early Christians were beheaded, crucified, and burned at the stake. Contemporary believers around the world today suffer persecution and death because they have chosen the identifying mark of the name of Jesus Christ.

Should we then choose baptism? The question lies couched in a statement made to Peter the night before Jesus was crucified: "Surely you are one of them" (Matt. 26:73).

Are we?

three

CELEBRATION
The Joy of a Public Witness

The man's testimony, read by the associate pastor, went as follows:

> A few years ago I had about given up on God, others, and even myself. I had little hope of ever returning to the better life I once lived or ever becoming the man I knew God wanted me to be. But God sought me out, and by his great mercy and love found me in the depths of sin. And there I confessed my sins and repented of my tragic condition. He forgave me, turned me around, and started me in the right direction. I have walked with God for over a year and want to ask you to rejoice with me in what God has done in my life.

At first, for a moment, silence filled the church, and then spontaneous praise and rejoicing erupted from the congregation. It lasted for only a few seconds—but it seemed like a long time—for this was the testimony of a new convert about to be baptized. The man stood in the water next to the pastor, who raised his right hand in the air, after placing his left hand on the man's shoulder, and said, "In the name of the Father, Son, and Holy Spirit, I baptize thee a Christian into the church of our Lord Jesus Christ." At that the pastor immersed the man in the water and raised him up again. The man's face, looking peaceful before baptism, was exultant afterward.[1]

Steve, the man being baptized, had traveled a long way to get to that Easter Sunday sunrise and baptism service. But the celebration was authentic, because every sin, every venture away from God, was nailed to the cross and no longer needed to be carried by Steve. It was a classic story of the joy of a public witness. Many in the congregation did not know Steve, but those who knew his story or heard his testimony that day shared in the celebration because another son came home. Think of all those who interceded in prayer and fasted meals for his salvation over many years. Think of those who prayed for him when he was a child or teen but died while he was still in sin and whose unanswered prayers on earth are now fulfilled in heaven. Indeed, a baptismal celebration is shared mutually among all redeemed sinners, for at another's baptism, they remember again that they, too, are also forgiven!

Baptism is truly a celebration for all Christians, but it celebrates something specifically if we are the ones being baptized.

First, baptism celebrates how far we've come as redeemed sons or daughters—as persons restored by Christ to their intended status with God. The change from what we once were to what we now are because of Christ is staggering. Once, we were ensnared by the awful trappings of sin; now we are liberated by the very law that used to condemn us. Once, we felt awkward at the idea of having Christ as a guest in our homes;

now we celebrate the thought of Christ's presence with total abandon, unashamed to have him where we live anytime.

First Peter summarizes the jolting shift that baptism celebrates by identifying our new status in Christ: "But you are a chosen people . . . God's special possession, that you may declare the praises of him who called you out of darkness into his wonderful light. Once you were not a people, but now you are the people of God; once you had not received mercy, but now you have received mercy" (2:9-10). What a remarkable transformation we celebrate at baptism; it is a "radical break with the old life and a radical incorporation into a new life, as radical an act as the death and resurrection of Christ himself."[2]

In Rom. 6 Paul lays great significance on Christ's baptism, death, and resurrection as a representation of what gives us reason to celebrate in our own baptism: "Or don't you know that all of us who were baptized in Christ Jesus were baptized into his death? We were therefore buried with him through baptism into death in order that, just as Christ was raised from the dead through the glory of the Father, we too may live a new life" (vv. 3-4). This passage is preceded by Paul's rhetorical question, "Shall we go on sinning so that grace may increase? By no means!" (vv. 1-2). Here Paul is making an effort to awaken the Romans to the grave mistake of living presumptuously with God, indifferent to both the beauty and burden of baptism in Christ.

Sin is not a phantom, a simple error of human judgment, for it willfully demeans the price Christ paid to be marked with the scars of the cross. For the celebration of baptism to be felt in all its wonder, the candidate must come to terms with Christ's death and resurrection. We celebrate at our baptism the victory of having died to sin so that we might live anew in Jesus Christ, the new Center of our devotion, who himself embodies the sinless life we strive to emulate. As Paul said, "The life [Christ] lives, he lives to God. In the same way, count yourselves dead to sin but alive to God in Christ Jesus. Therefore do not let sin reign in your mortal body so that you obey its evil desires" (vv. 10-12).

This passage underscores why we celebrate our own baptism: as Christians we take personal responsibility for our new journey. Baptism is not done by proxy; we own our own place in the water. It is a sacramental event worth celebrating because "the Christian is called to become in his daily living what he already is 'in Christ', to work out the implications of what his baptism meant . . . , as the circumcised Israelite needed to 'make good' his circumcision by a life of obedience within the covenant."[3]

In becoming Christians we did not become marionettes, mere puppets on strings controlled at a distance by a manipulative god. Rather, we celebrate because we linked up with the redeemer God who rejoices over a new relationship with us and then, amazingly, asks us to rise from the baptismal water and "make good" on our life choices. Any life in which sin is conquered is a good life worth celebrating. Paul wrote, "Continue to work out your salvation with fear and trembling, for it is God who works in you to will and to act in order to fulfill his good purpose" (Phil. 2:12-13).

Second, baptism celebrates our acceptance into the family of God. As cited earlier, God loved us before our conversion, when we still lived in sin. Indeed, God's love for us is not based on our salvation or baptism. He just loves us! But baptism is not about love in the sense of

God's favor or grace. Baptism is a rite of entry or initiation into God's family, marking our acceptance within the community of believers.

Two passages of Scripture demonstrate the uniqueness of baptism as a means of entry into the fellowship of the church, also called the body of Christ. Paul addressed the Corinthian church in his first letter to them: "For we were all baptized by one Spirit so as to form one body—whether Jews or Gentiles, slave or free—and we were all given the one Spirit to drink" (12:13). Baptism recognizes that we are spiritually regenerated (made new in Christ) by the Holy Spirit and united with Christ as part of his body. But baptism celebrates even more: in Christ there is no social, racial, or cultural distinction. More directly, once we are "in Christ" as his forgiven and adopted children, we are truly "in" and belong to him. This is what baptism celebrates.

Paul said it similarly to the Galatians: "In Christ Jesus you are all children of God through faith, for all of you who were baptized into Christ have clothed yourselves with Christ. There is neither Jew nor Gentile, neither slave nor free, nor is there male and female, for you are all one in Christ Jesus. . . . and heirs according to the promise" (3:26-29).

Unity in Christ also transcends gender and ethnic distinctions and expects that a Christian's holy life will prohibit the tragic and destructive excesses that toleration of these barriers creates. That is, there must be no barriers in the church. We are accepted just as we are. Now for the hard question: does it actually work out like this? When you get baptized and become part of a church fellowship, are the dividing walls of hostility due to racial, ethnic, gender, social, and cultural distinctions completely removed?

Unfortunately we know that the answer is no. No church is a paradise, completely free from the residue of centuries of prejudice and indifference to the differences that trouble Christians even after conversion and baptism.

These verses describe not merely the hope but also the biblical expectation of a holy God. God believes that those who bear the mark of baptism can and must rise above the petty divisions that often plague his children. How is this possible? By remembering that baptism celebrates a giving up of the prejudicial ways we used to think about people and a dying out to the self-centered ways we used to think about ourselves. Instead we choose to respect and value one another's differences. This is possible because the church, in all its diversity, *represents* Christ as its head and *presents* Christ to the yet unsaved world.

We have a lot to celebrate as Christ strengthens us to make the church an even stronger witness!

four

HERITAGE

Contemporary Wesleyan Perspectives

Although my mom's dad was an electrician with a garage full of tools and my dad's dad was a dairy farmer with horticultural talents, I inherited none of their mechanical, technical, and electrical skills (or tools). Yet totaling both sides of my family there were ten Methodist, Wesleyan, and Nazarene ministers prior to me. A person's heritage is like an extended family album revealing physical, cultural, religious, and social information, disclosing resemblances and differences.

Just as family members with the same name and bloodline differ, so do churches in the same tradition. The following contemporary descriptions highlight similarities and differences on baptism among churches within the Wesleyan tradition. These churches all trace their theological identity to John Wesley, an Anglican (Church of England) minister of the 1700s, who initially never intended to start a separate denominational tradition.

The United Methodist Church believes that baptism is a sign of the new birth and a declaration and "mark" that distinguishes Christians from those not baptized. The church does maintain that a person can be saved without being baptized. Methodists believe that baptism is a sacrament that celebrates God's initiative in establishing a covenant relationship. Sprinkling, pouring, and immersion are acceptable modes of baptism.[1]

United Methodists do not practice rebaptism but instead offer a ritual for the "reaffirmation of baptismal vows, which implies that, while God remains faithful to God's half of the covenant, we are not always faithful to our promises. Our half of the covenant is to confess Christ as our Savior, trust in his grace, serve him as Lord in the church, and carry out his mission against evil, injustice, and oppression."[2]

The Wesleyan Church affirms water baptism as a sacrament that is ordained as a means of grace through which "[God] works within us to quicken, strengthen and confirm our faith. . . . It is a symbol of the new covenant of grace and signifies acceptance of the benefits of the atonement of Jesus Christ. By means of this sacrament, believers declare their faith in Jesus Christ as Savior."[3] Like all holiness churches that practice baptism, Wesleyans view this sacrament as a sign of God's grace; they do not believe salvation is in the water.

The Free Methodist Church views baptism as a "sacrament of the church, commanded by our Lord, signifying acceptance of the benefits of the atonement of Jesus Christ to be administered to believers, as declaration of their faith in Jesus Christ as Savior."[4]

The Church of Christ in Christian Union states, "We believe that Christ and His apostles ordained two ordinances to be practiced by His Church: water baptism and the Lord's supper. We insist on no exclusive method or mode of baptism or of partaking the Lord's supper. Let each be fully persuaded in his own mind. These ordinances are outward symbols, teaching of the inner life, the faith, and the hope of believers."[5]

The Christian and Missionary Alliance Church, while strongly shunning the baptism of infants or children prior to the age of accountability, strongly affirms believer's baptism. "Baptism is simply an outward demonstration of that which has taken place inwardly. Baptism is not an initiation rite into Christianity. . . . It is symbolic of joining with Christ in His death, burial and resurrection for one's sin. . . . Therefore, the Christian and Missionary Alliance believes that baptism is reserved for the person who already believes in Jesus Christ for the forgiveness of his or her sin."[6]

The Church of God (Anderson, Indiana), birthed and nurtured within the American Holiness Movement in the late eighteenth century, locates its theological roots within Wesleyan pietism. The Church of God affirms water baptism only by immersion. "Baptism is a first step in the life of the Christian convert,"[7] and it is a "witness to the new believer's regeneration in Christ and inclusion in the family of God."[8]

The Assemblies of God churches "believe baptism in water is to follow salvation (acceptance of Christ and His forgiveness of our sins) as demonstrated in the New Testament. For this reason we urge all new converts to follow the biblical pattern of water baptism in obedience to Christ."[9]

The Salvation Army, while an ardent proponent of Wesleyan holiness, does not recognize any sacrament, including baptism or the Lord's Supper. Sacraments are viewed as unnecessary, not wrong. Modern-day Salvationists avoid sacraments for the following reasons: (1) they are mere symbols that may become rituals; (2) they don't change the heart or life; and (3) "Jesus did not intend to create sacramental ceremonies and there is little . . . in the Bible to support sacraments."[10] New members are called soldiers, and the equivalent of a baptism ceremony is held that does not involve water and is not considered sacramental. Members are allowed to be baptized in another church.

The Church of the Nazarene includes a statement on baptism in its Articles of Faith:

> We believe that Christian baptism, commanded by our Lord, is a sacrament signifying acceptance of the benefits of the atonement of Jesus Christ, to be administered to believers. . . .
>
> Baptism being a symbol of the new covenant, young children may be baptized, upon request of parents or guardians who shall give assurance for them of necessary Christian training.
>
> Baptism may be administered by sprinkling, pouring, or immersion, according to the choice of the applicant.[11]

While nothing is said specifically about infant baptism, Nazarenes affirm both infant baptism and dedication with corollary rituals in their denominational *Manual.*

Nearly three centuries before these contemporary views surfaced, John and Charles Wesley were students at Oxford University. Methodical in their mutual accountability and Bible study, fellow students derisively called them Methodists, and hence the name stuck—both for them and the denomination that eventually emerged. Indeed, Great Britain, Ireland, and the United States witnessed the effect of a social and spiritual reformation brought about by the Methodist Church through the preaching of John and the hymn writing of Charles.

John Wesley believed that the sacraments, including baptism, were a "means of grace" to the participant. In his sermon "The Means of Grace," Wesley wrote, "By 'means of grace' I understand outward signs, words, or actions, ordained of God, and appointed for this end, to be the ordinary channels whereby he might convey to men preventing, justifying, or sanctifying grace."[12] By receiving the Lord's Supper or being baptized one does not *become* a Christian, because in the same sermon Wesley adds that "the use of all means whatever will never atone for one sin; that it is the blood of Christ alone, whereby any sinner can be reconciled to God; there being no other propitiation [or way of having God's wrath turned away] for our sins."[13]

We are saved by Christ alone, and a sacrament is a strong bond or covenant between us and God that identifies the grace that was so freely given and that continues to be given. A sacrament is a reminder of the price Christ paid for our salvation and is visible evidence of our participation in the ongoing grace of God.

By comparison, the Lord's Supper is offered frequently, while the baptism of adults is done once and is not usually repeated. The means of grace are the *practices* that promote the development of the holy life. Sometimes we may think that because baptism is a singular event, it must not be as important a sacrament as the Lord's Supper. But Wesley believed that "grace is conveyed through that sacrament [baptism] also, when it is accompanied by faith, and thus it may properly be called a means of grace."[14] The means or ways of experiencing the grace of God were, for Wesley, not intended as an open door to whatever seemed expedient. Christ must be central to the means itself, so Wesley held that prayer, the sacraments of baptism and the Lord's Supper, the Word (both Scripture and sermon), fasting, and Christian fellowship were authentic means of grace.

Wesley did not believe that the sacraments transferred grace or that they could save us or forgive sins. Again in "The Means of Grace" sermon, Wesley wrote, "'By grace are ye saved:' Ye are saved from your sins, from the guilt and power thereof, ye are restored to the favor and image of God, not for any works, merits, or deservings of yours, but by the free grace, the mere mercy of God, through the merits of his well-beloved Son: Ye are thus saved, not by any power, wisdom, or strength, which is in you."[15] The essence of grace is that God does for us what we cannot do for ourselves.

Grace is God's undeserved mercy when we are guilty of sin, and it is also the way the Holy Spirit delivers us from the grip or power of sin. For Wesley, both views of grace are accomplished in the atonement, or what Christ did for us on the cross. The sacraments (and other means of grace) are the "means by which the Holy Spirit applies the atonement of Christ in all its ramifications."[16]

Wesley's ministry 250 years ago greatly impacted the religious climate in the United States and ultimately sacramental practice in my own denomination, the Church of the Nazarene. But not all early Nazarenes embraced baptism as a necessary means of grace.

My paternal grandfather, the dairy farmer mentioned earlier in this chapter, donated five hundred dollars in the early 1950s to help remodel the church I mentioned in the first chapter. However, he had one stipulation: his money must go to some part of the building program *not* associated with the baptistery. Grandfather greatly admired John Wesley but parted with him on baptism.

Thus his gift came through when my dad said he would apply the amount toward landscaping.

Actually, my grandfather was not alone. Born in 1874, he was a product of the American Holiness Movement. The Holiness Movement was definitely a child of nineteenth-century revivalism and represented a potent doctrinal departure from classic Wesleyan practices in Methodist churches in the United States. Many conservative Christians at that time shunned what they perceived as more structured and formal religion, particularly the kind found in Methodist and other mainline churches. The fervor of camp-meeting life was in full swing in those days throughout the southern and eastern United States. Revivalism was all about the fulfillment of heartfelt religion. Personal revival was no doubt the intent of many a seeker, whether at a prayer altar in church or a mourner's bench at the end of a sawdust trail on camp-meeting circuits.

Though Wesley's meticulous attention to liturgy and sacramental theology were notable elements in his own practice of worship and were clearly evident in American Methodist churches, Methodism seemed cold and formal to many of the emerging holiness groups who spurned anything that lacked the feel of spontaneity and life. It is no surprise that the concept of sacrament and even the use of the word "liturgy" were minimized, not because they were perceived as evil, but because they were without fervency.

Baptism and Communion were practiced with some regularity due to the heritage spawned by Wesley (and Francis Asbury in the United States) and the pervasive influence of the Methodist Church. Baptism was observed as a public testimony, and the Lord's Supper was viewed as a memorial. However, a sacrament "was not perceived as a means whereby *present* grace is conveyed, except in the sense that simply remembering the Lord's sacrifice is a helpful aid to Christian living."[17]

Baptism as a sacrament was incorporated into many Wesleyan churches owing largely to Wesley's influence, although most holiness groups at that time did not have a well-developed sacramental theology. Early church fathers centuries prior to Wesley were influenced by Augustine and the Apostles' Creed. As Wesleyan churches practiced, honored, and better understood the sacraments in the light of history and the Apostles' Creed, a new level of personal accountability was embraced.

five

ACCOUNTABILITY

The Shape of Community among Believers

On a crisp fall day Ken,* a pastor from out of town, was up early for a morning run before leaving his motel to attend a ministry conference. But first he had to find a secure place to put his watch and billfold. There was no safe in the room, and there were few other options. Without much thought, he stuffed his valuables between the mattresses as far as he could reach.

An hour later, he easily retrieved his billfold, but the watch was farther back. When he located it, his hand brushed against something. What else did he put there? Searching again he felt the edge of a magazine. Pulling it out slowly he realized it was probably a porn magazine.

He was right. So there he was, about three hundred miles from home, with no one around. Who would ever know? What came to his mind first was not that he was a Christian, married, or an ordained minister or that he

---

*Not his real name.

was baptized many years earlier. What first came to Ken's mind was a disarmingly effective children's chorus:

> *O be careful little eyes what you see;*
> *O be careful little eyes what you see;*
> *For the Father up above is looking down in love,*
> *So be careful little eyes what you see.*[1]

Why that little song? Why not something profound?

Then he remembered: he first heard that children's song in Sunday school at a church long ago. Many years had passed, but the depth of spiritual formation contained in those simple lyrics, profound enough indeed, remained in his memory.[2]

This clearly illustrates the duty of the church, even if in an elementary manner. It is the biblical and missional obligation of the body of Christ to educate and bring to spiritual maturity all within its reach. And it also identifies the ethical and moral standard to which all believers must rise. Community among believers within the church is shaped by mutual accountability between newer converts who are candidates for baptism and those who've been in the church for years. We all have to take up our responsibility.

Accountability is not designed to be fun. Nobody harvests a crop in the field, defends a dissertation, or represents a client in court without being accountable. So it is with any candidate for baptism and the church that offers this sacrament. In Ken's case, he was wisely shaped by teachers, local churches, and a larger Christian culture—all of which understood they had a mission to be accountable to him by instilling biblical truth and providing an atmosphere where he could mature. Moreover, that morning in the motel he had his own duty to shun evil.

Paul's great passage in Col. 3:1-12 is a bold and clear call rich with the baptismal metaphor he so often employed. If a church practices water-immersion baptism, candidates will likely change into different clothes suitable for the occasion. After baptism, they'll dress again to go home. Paul links this change of garments—taking off one set of clothes and putting on another set after baptism—with putting off the old nature of sin and putting on the new nature of righteousness. He speaks symbolically as if a person dies to one way of life by being buried under water and then rises to a new way of ethical behavior and living in Christ. Baptism marks the transition from the old life of sinful practice to the new life in Christ.

Notice the striking images he uses in this passage:

- "Since, then, you have been raised with Christ" (v. 1).
- "For you died, and your life is now hidden with Christ in God" (v. 3).
- "Put to death, therefore, whatever belongs to your earthly nature: sexual immorality, impurity, lust, evil desires and greed, which is idolatry" (v. 5).
- "Therefore, as God's chosen people, holy and dearly loved, clothe yourselves with compassion, kindness, humility, gentleness and patience" (v. 12).

Most helpful for understanding the rigors of personal accountability that candidates and churches must shoulder are these verses: "Do not lie to each other, since you have taken off your old self with its practices and have put on the new self, which is being renewed in knowledge in the image of its Creator" (vv. 9-10).

Another translation of the second part of v. 10 reads, "The new self . . . is being refitted all the time for closer knowledge, so the image of the God who created it is its pattern" (KNOX). This verse catches the flavor of the ongoing accountability in which we allow God to daily measure and refit us so his image may be clearly evident.

A helpful corollary text is Gal. 3:27: "For all of you who were baptized into Christ *have clothed yourselves with Christ*" (emphasis added).

Thomas Hamerken, born about 1380 in Kempen, Germany, is better remembered as Thomas à Kempis and author of the devotional classic *The Imitation of Christ*. In a simple but eloquent prayer he speaks to the issue of being personally accountable to God in the light of his own frailties: "But because I am as yet weak in love, and imperfect in virtue, I have need to be strengthened and comforted by thee; visit me therefore often, and instruct me with all holy discipline. Set me free from evil passions, and heal my heart of all inordinate affections; that being inwardly cured and thoroughly cleansed, I may be made fit to love, courageous to suffer, steady to persevere."[3]

Through the discipline of accountability we are liberated from seductive attitudes and affections with which we once dressed ourselves in spiritual darkness, grabbing any old thing we could find—the best rags sin could offer. Turning away from those sad days, now we ask God to outfit us with an attitude and lifestyle that reflects his holy image and our faithful intent. This is the new direction that our being accountable to God presents.

In healthy churches, a climate of interdependency is created between baptismal candidates and a small group, the congregation at large, and a pastor or mentor. Candidates are expected to attend a class on baptism. Faithful church attendance will be expected before and after baptism. The congregation, on the other hand, will respond with prayerful support by hearing the baptismal covenant—including the Apostles' Creed—being read in a public worship service. Part of the covenant contains these words:

> The earliest and simplest statement of Christian belief, into which you now come to be baptized, is the Apostles' Creed, which reads as follows:
>
> "I believe in God the Father Almighty, Maker of heaven and earth;
>
> "And in Jesus Christ, His only Son, our Lord; who was conceived by the Holy Ghost, born of the Virgin Mary, suffered under Pontius Pilate, was crucified, dead, and buried; He descended into hell; the third day He rose again from the dead; He ascended into heaven, and sits at the right hand of God the Father Almighty; from thence He shall come to judge the quick and the dead.
>
> "I believe in the Holy Ghost, the holy Church of Jesus Christ, the communion of saints, the forgiveness of sins, the resurrection of the body, and the life everlasting."
>
> Will you be baptized into this faith? If so, answer, "I will." . . .
>
> Do you acknowledge Jesus Christ as your personal Savior, and do you realize that He saves you now? . . .
>
> Will you obey God's holy will and keep His commandments, walking in them all the days of your life?"[4]

The Apostles' Creed, no light matter to any Christian, concisely frames the scope of Christian belief and establishes the parameters within which the church functions theologically. That the church agrees publicly to this creed at baptism attests to its value for accountability. The exacting affirmations in this creed would be expected of any church whose order and discipline are founded in Scripture.

But the emerging New Testament church, and its Christian successors for several centuries, did not view water baptism as the end point in holy living. Rather, baptism was the initiation into God's family, celebrating a new beginning for the new candidate. As the young Christian church continually sought to distinguish itself from a pervasively pagan culture, it faced increasing challenges. The road to and from baptism was not intended to be trouble-free.

As early as the second century, the *Apostolic Tradition* of Hippolytus of Rome "depicts baptism not as a momentary rite but, rather, as part of a long process of initiation into the Christian community."[5] Those who were admitted as candidates for baptism were required to take a three-year period of instruction in Old Testament scripture. Some were summarily denied admission if their profession or lifestyle suggested immoral behavior, and even soldiers were eliminated due to their alliance with the pagan state.

For those who finally reached the moment of baptism, the minister immersed candidates three times during the reading of an earlier but similar version of our Apostles' Creed, following questions on matters of belief requiring the candidates' agreement. In the early church everyone took this ritual seriously: "The Christian life required conversion, re-formation, and discipline on the part of the believer. Baptism was not some magical ablution. It required response on the part of the recipient and a new orientation of one's life. As Christ rose from the tomb on Easter as the resurrected Lord, so these

41

initiates emerged from the baptismal waters as new and redeemed people."[6]

A church is at its best as a community of faith when it freely loves the most wretched outcast hungry for sin and wisely counsels the most ardent candidate eager for baptism.

six

REFLECTION
Considering Important Issues

When the office secretary told the pastor he had the wrong card for the ceremony the next Sunday, he responded that he meant to get a blue one, since the baby was a boy.

"You have the right color, but this card is for infant *baptism*, not infant dedication. We don't do infant baptisms, remember?"

Her reminder was given politely, simply intending to jog the pastor's memory. So he explained that the church did indeed have four rituals, including one for infant baptism and another for infant dedication. She was surprised. This good secretary, not an attendee of the church where she worked, was a faithful Southern Baptist.

Doctrinally, her denomination does not endorse infant baptism or any other mode of water baptism except immersion. The pastor also mentioned that his church, which belongs to the Wesleyan tradition, practices baptism by immersion, pouring, or sprinkling, depending on the preference of the candidate or, in this case, the parents.[1]

With the exception of the Salvation Army and the Society of Friends (Quakers), baptism has been adopted as a sacrament by most Christian faiths since the early church. Yet people differ on the mode of baptism and on the issue of infant baptism. Even Wesleyans do not agree on every point. What we must do is avoid the extremes of unthinking loyalty to our own opinion, on the one hand, and of demanding denominational conformity from neighboring faiths, on the other.

Thus we recognize and respect the disparity of views, especially on infant baptism within the Wesleyan tradition. Among the churches with theological ties to John Wesley, there is nearly an even split on this issue. Churches that practice infant baptism include the Wesleyan Church, the United Methodist Church, the Free Methodist Church, and the Church of the Nazarene, while those that shun it include the Christian and Missionary Alliance, the Church of God (Anderson, Indiana), the Assemblies of God, and the Salvation Army.

This difference over infant or child baptism seems to depend on whether or not there is scriptural evidence for this practice in the early church. Creedal statements from contemporary churches within the Wesleyan tradition read the same scriptures and arrive at different opinions. Those churches that endorse infant baptism strongly emphasize prevenient grace, in which God takes the initiative to offer salvation well before any of us seek it; this is especially so with infants and children before the age of accountability. Those that do not endorse infant baptism believe that it should come only after a child is old enough to comprehend salvation and articulate his or her own experience by faith.

The United Methodist Church, the Assemblies of God, the Church of the Nazarene, and several other churches offer dedication as an alternative to infant baptism. Churches in the Wesleyan tradition that practice baptism would agree that something more than ritual, but less than salvation, happens in the water. Other churches, such as the Salvation Army, do not practice baptism (or Communion), since they do not view the sacraments as essential to salvation.

With that said, let us turn to Scripture itself.

First, how is baptism related to salvation and getting into heaven? Matthew's gospel records John the Baptist's message: "'Repent, for the kingdom of heaven has come near.' . . . People went out to him from Jerusalem. . . . Confessing their sins, they were baptized by him in the Jordan River" (3:2, 5-6). On the day of Pentecost Peter preached, "Repent and be baptized, every one of you, in the name of Jesus Christ for the forgiveness of your sins" (Acts 2:38).

David Young suggests that the typical pattern of salvation in the New Testament is for repentance, confession, and the forgiveness of sins to lead to the reception of the Holy Spirit, which is the first evidence of being saved, followed by baptism.[2] However, infants are baptized as a recognition that God's prevenient grace is already at work in their lives. This is an exception to the view that salvation (as morally responsible persons experience it) must always precede baptism.

Jesus said to Nicodemus, "No one can enter the kingdom of God unless they are born of water and the Spirit" (John 3:5). But "water" in the context of John's gospel reveals that "it is a symbol of the old order of the Law with its ritual of baptisms . . . and cleansings.

. . . It is as though [Jesus] said: 'Nicodemus, begin where you are. But fulfillment, life, the solving of your innermost problem will come only with birth from above, the birth of the Spirit!'"[3]

Three other times in John 3 Jesus states that a person receives eternal life through believing, without mention of baptism (vv. 3, 15-16). Verse 16 is a great reminder that heaven is assured by faith, not baptism. Clearly we are forgiven our sins when, by faith, we confess and repent. Baptism is not minimized by these verses; yet neither is it elevated above repentance and confession. John Wesley, an ardent proponent of water baptism, believed that this sacrament was not necessary for salvation, since "if it were, every Quaker must be damned, which I can in no wise believe."[4]

Second, what does the Bible say about the mode or way baptism is administered? Scripture does not suggest a *required* mode for water baptism, nor require one of us. By implication or assumed practice, immersion, pouring, and sprinkling are all cited. Ralph Martin states that "the Greek terms for 'baptize' [and] 'baptism' mean strictly 'douse' or 'saturating'; and there is a lack of decisiveness as to the mode of baptism from the use of the language employed."[5]

John Wesley, in "A Treatise on Baptism," seems quite specific in his belief that Scripture is *un*specific about the mode: "Baptism is performed by washing, dipping, or sprinkling the person, in the name of the Father, Son, and Holy Ghost, who is hereby devoted to the ever-blessed Trinity. . . . it is not determined in Scripture in which of these ways it shall be done, neither by any express precept, nor by any such example as clearly proves it; nor by the force or meaning of the word *baptize*."[6]

It was Wesley's conviction that John's and Jesus' baptisms had similarities and differences and that neither dipping nor immersion could be conclusively proven from Scripture in either of their ministries. Wesley's point is, "For the words *baptize* and *baptism* do not necessarily imply *dipping*, but are used in other senses in several places."[7] Wesley observed that part of the issue was the lack of water, depending on the baptismal site, and that the original language for "baptism" sometimes referred to washing or cleansing and not submerging. Thus, regarding the day of Pentecost, when three thousand were converted and baptized by Peter and other disciples in Jerusalem (and five thousand at a later time), Wesley noted the absence of a sufficient body of water, making it improbable that immersion was practiced, leaving sprinkling and pouring as the options.[8]

"To sum up all, the manner of baptizing . . . is not determined in Scripture. There is no command for one rather than the other. There is no example from which we can conclude for dipping rather than sprinkling. There are probable examples of both."[9] One creedal statement reads, "Baptism may be administered by sprinkling, pouring, or immersion, according to the choice of the applicant."[10]

The opinions of the writers cited are not intended to minimize those of Christ-followers outside the Wesleyan tradition. Rather, they are mentioned as a way to better understand baptism in the light of Scripture. The words of J. Kenneth Grider provide a helpful recap:

> The mode of baptism was not made altogether clear in Scripture. Sprinkling is only possibly alluded to. . . . Immersion might be implied by the "buried with [Christ] in baptism" reference in Rom. 6:4. Pouring

might be suggested because twice in Acts 2 (vv. 17-18), reference is made to the prophecy in Joel 2:28 about the Spirit being poured out; and surely Pentecost fulfilled that prophecy, as well as those in Matt. 3:11-12 and Acts 1:4-5.[11]

The important issue is not how much water we use to get baptized but whether we follow the practice of Jesus by being baptized. Alan Richardson observes that "it was Jesus himself who first taught that his own death was a baptism that could and must be shared by all who would participate in the Messianic salvation."[12]

Third, should infants be baptized or dedicated? The infant baptism debate is summarized by considering two respected scholars. George Allen Turner argues *against* infant baptism, citing the baptism of the Philippian jailer and his household of Acts 16, who "became believers between midnight and dawn; were sleeping infants aroused to participate in the baptism? . . . it seems an unwarranted assumption."[13] Grider, however, cites the same passage *in favor* of infant baptism: "A 'household' included any children . . . of the household's head. . . . in an era when children could not be planned as they can be in our day, it would have been mathematically improbable that in these households there were no children who had not as yet reached the age of accountability."[14]

The *Manual* of the Church of the Nazarene allows for both viewpoints, having rituals for infant baptism and infant dedication. This denomination values both practices for their individual merit and to accommodate unresolvable but respected differences. Because it allows for both rites, this church's approach calls for closer attention.

Unlike baptism, along with the absence of water, the Nazarene dedication ritual is not identified as a sacrament in the church's *Manual*.[15] Also, the dedication ritual, to borrow from the thinking of Rob Staples, lacks historical precedent and New Testament support.[16] Yet God's name is invoked in both rituals, and the questions put to the parents are similar in either protocol. But the following statement in the infant *baptism* ritual is absent in the infant *dedication* ritual: "The sacrament of baptism is the sign and seal of the new covenant of grace. While we do not hold that baptism imparts the regenerating grace of God, we do believe that Christian baptism signifies for this young child God's acceptance within the community of Christian faith on the basis of prevenient grace. It anticipates his (her) personal confession of faith in Jesus Christ."[17]

Baptism in Scripture was intended to honor the beauty, wonder, and awe of what Christ Jesus did for us in his own baptism, death, and resurrection. Thus infant baptism is a sacrament acknowledging prevenient grace in Christ—the DNA of God's intention to cover by the blood of Christ those children who are too young to understand. Though parents must raise their baptized or dedicated children to revere God, when children reach the age of moral responsibility, they still must confess their sins and seek Christ as their Savior.[18]

For H. Ray Dunning, a Church of the Nazarene theologian, "there is solid basis for infant baptism as a ritual that bears witness to the reality of prevenient grace."[19] He suggests that it attests to an "already existing 'covering of [Christ's] Blood.'"[20] Moreover, he maintains that the church's *Manual* allows for such an interpretation not only in its "article of faith on baptism" but also in its "twofold ritual pertaining to the 'dedication' or 'baptism' of infants."[21]

To be fair, neither ritual detracts from the other, for the purpose of both is to engage sincere parents in the holy calling of bringing their little ones to maturity in Christ.

seven

RESPONSIBILITY

What's a Parent *Really* to Do?

There is no question that the baptism or dedication of your child is clearly about your *child*. He or she is the one being presented to the Lord. But this event is also about *you*—your feelings, your interpretation of what this ceremony means, and your decision to proceed with it. Even more, this sacred event has eternal significance because of how you will raise your child in the years to come in response to the commitments you will make before God, your church, and your minister. Plus, your child may be so young that he or she will have little or no memory of being baptized or dedicated. So how can your decision best serve your child?

First, remember that technical jargon or doctrinal differences must not deter your decision to move forward. Yes, you must weigh the issues and seek counsel to gain all the clarity you can. But you are essentially making a decision to present your child to the Lord. If you've read the other chapters in this booklet, you know how easy it would be to get mired in theological language, differences of opinion, and even doctrinal disagreements between denominations. Your pastor can assist you with these matters. But ultimately, presenting your child to the Lord is a clear way of honoring God and his desire for the child's salvation.

Second, you must come to terms with whether you will have your child baptized or dedicated. This worthy issue deserves your patient consideration. One creedal statement declares that young children are covered under the atonement:[1] "The Atonement is graciously efficacious [effective] for the salvation of those incapable of moral responsibility and for the children in innocency but is efficacious for the salvation of those who reach the age of responsibility only when they repent and believe."[2] God's grace is large enough to be effective for infants and little children who are too innocent to be morally accountable for sin. However, even before your child becomes old enough to understand right from wrong, your duty will be to teach the importance of repentance from sin and about faith in Christ that leads to salvation.

Prevenient grace, or grace that is given to everyone at birth, covers the innocent and is at work in young children. Without question John Wesley ardently supported infant baptism: "But the grand question is, Who are the proper subjects of baptism? grown persons only, or infants also? . . . I shall, First, lay down the grounds of infant baptism, taken from Scripture, reason, and primitive, universal practice."[3] His sermon "A Treatise on Baptism" continues with methodical support for this ritual.

As mentioned in chapter 4, Wesleyan denominations in the United States have had to minister within a cultural and religious setting different from Wesley's. This distinct setting, influenced largely by frontier individualism and camp-meeting revivalism, diminished the role of the church itself, with a resulting loss of sacramental identity. Today, with patient pastoral instruction, perhaps there can be a reconsideration of what the New Testament says about including children in baptism. Hopefully, as H. Ray Dunning observes, "a genuine validity can be attached to infant baptism if it is seen as the induction of the child into the covenant community. . . . It might, in fact, militate against the loss of children from the church by guarding against the church becoming spectators until the child experiences an adult conversion."[4]

Jesse Middendorf's *Church Rituals Handbook* offers a helpful perspective on infant baptism:

> For those who choose infant baptism, many churches hold that there is a significant moment of grace involved, not that we convey grace in the sacrament, but that we proclaim the prevenient grace of God that covers this child from the time of birth, and even before. . . . In this rite . . . we believe that God has incorporated this child into His Body by prevenient grace. But we are not determining for this child what his (her) choices will be later in life.[5]

You may prefer dedication, but infant baptism is also endorsed by several churches as biblically and theologically authentic.

Third, the covenant you will make at baptism or dedication includes your willingness to do all you can to raise your child as a Christian. You must make this decision on behalf of your child, since he or she is too small to understand or have a say in the matter. Clearly a child's faith decision is a personal decision. Unfortunately some parents reason that a child's religious instruction should wait until he or she is older or perhaps be up to the child entirely. However, parents make other decisions for their child about diet, education, medical care, safety, and personal development. They make these decisions because they instinctively know it is right and want to do what is best for their child. How much more important is it to influence the child's spiritual and eternal direction! Keep in mind, in presenting your little one to the Lord *you* are not assuring his or her salvation. God's wondrous grace does that at birth. You are simply saying you'll do your part as a faithful parent; when children reach the age of moral responsibility, the salvation decision is theirs.

Fourth, in the years following baptism or dedication your church will come to mean more to your child than you now realize. In 1752 Wesley wrote "Serious Thoughts Concerning Godfathers and Godmothers," in which he observed that the ancient church provided two or more sponsors. Wesley asked, "What then is your part, [you,] who are sponsors for the child? . . . 'You shall call upon him to hear sermons, and shall provide that he may learn the [Apostles'] Creed, the Lord's Prayer, and the Ten Commandments, and all other things which a Christian ought to know and believe to his soul's health; and that this child may be virtuously brought up, to lead a godly and a Christian life.'"[6]

As a part of the church, your ministry—whether or not it's similar to Wesley's—may be that of loving support to any child or youth, even if he or she is not yours. In today's more complicated social climate you must be careful to obtain parental approval before assuming any mentoring role with children. Once clearance is given, it is important to model Christ during counseling, home visits, religious teaching, and all other aspects of contact. In particular, Sunday school teachers and children's and youth workers have an added responsibility for communicating with parents and maintaining appropriate relationships with minors at all levels. It is very important that children learn to build relationships with adults other than their own parents.

I should know. Ned Thompson was not my dad. He was in charge of the Sunday school at the church I attended as a child (see chap. 1). Ned took a special interest in me. He was an electrician with his own business, family, and life. But for reasons I could not fully comprehend at the time, he invested himself in me. I'm embarrassed to admit it, but I got in a fistfight with a kid during class one Sunday. I was about eleven. The teacher was out of the room, and before I knew it, another boy and I were fighting. It wasn't all that bad, but one of us got a bloody nose, and both of us had blood on our shirts. The teacher came in, settled us down, made us apologize, and that was that.

But when class was over and we walked out into the larger children's department room, there was Mr. Thompson. I can't quite put in words what his face looked like, but it was a mixture of sadness and affirmation at the same time. I felt safe looking at his face because he did not look angry. I also felt bad for my part. He looked at both of us, and the other boy walked on by. So Uncle Ned, as he let us call him, walked over to me, put his arm around my shoulder, and hugged me. He motioned for us to walk outside, and it seemed like a long time before he spoke.

Finally he said, "Well, Jim, there's two things. First, I've got the goods on you, and you will need to tell your dad about this so I won't have to." Then he turned to face me and placed both hands on my shoulders. "Jim," he continued, "I want you to know that I like you just like you are. You can do better than this, can't you? But you will always be liked by me. Don't forget that." I didn't know what to say.

He motioned for us to go back inside, and his face and manner remained gracious, affirming, and equable. I will never forget that face. And I think that should be the posture of anyone seeking to mentor children and youth, whether that role is filled by a thoughtful sponsor, a loving parent, or a healthy church. Like Uncle Ned, a wise and caring mentor corrects and encourages, holding little ones accountable in appropriate ways and offering forbearance in every way.

Conclusion

Baptism was defined in the New Testament by its identification with something fresh. By the act of his own baptism, Jesus introduced a kingdom movement, a different way of looking at loyalty to his heavenly Father. It was neither rule based nor shame based, as was the prevailing teaching of the Pharisees. It was allegiance based. Jesus' baptism was his way of saying, "There is Someone greater than I, and I will embrace his cause and die for it."

Such radical identification as this was unheard of, but then, so would be Jesus' miracles and parables. Principled and devout, Jesus viewed his public baptism as more than mere display: it was meant to be the pattern for his followers. Baptism identified Jesus' selfless and public commitment to God.

This is what Jesus intends baptism to be for us—loyalty to a new identity, a new direction. Your baptism is a way of saying publicly, "I am yours, Lord. I will follow you." The presentation of your infant or child in baptism or dedication affirms, "To the best of my ability I will raise this child to the honor and glory of God."

Such a view of baptism is just as challenging and necessary today as it was in the first century.

Notes

Chapter 1

1. *Webster's Seventh New Collegiate Dictionary*, s.v. "sacrament."

2. Ralph P. Martin, *Worship in the Early Church* (1964; repr., Grand Rapids: Eerdmans, 2001), 87.

3. J. Kenneth Grider, *A Wesleyan-Holiness Theology* (Kansas City: Beacon Hill Press of Kansas City, 1994), 497.

4. A. M. Hills, *Fundamental Christian Theology,* abr. ed. (Pasadena, CA: C. J. Kinne, 1932), 515.

5. Michael Lodahl, *The Story of God: A Narrative Theology* (Kansas City: Beacon Hill Press of Kansas City, 2008), 178.

6. C. S. Lewis, *The Problem of Pain* (New York: Macmillan, 1962), 93, 95.

7. Rudolf Otto, *The Idea of the Holy* (New York: Oxford University Press, 1958), 26.

8. Lodahl, *Story of God,* 178.

9. Author's personal story.

10. Lodahl, *Story of God*, 178.

11. John Newton, "Amazing Grace," in *Worship in Song* (Kansas City: Lillenas, 1972), 212.

Chapter 2

1. William M. Greathouse, *Romans 1–8*, New Beacon Bible Commentary (Kansas City: Beacon Hill Press of Kansas City, 2008), 179. Quotation within quotation from Robert Jewett, *Romans: A Commentary*, Hermeneia (Minneapolis: Fortress, 2007), 398.

2. Rob L. Staples, *Outward Sign and Inward Grace: The Place of Sacraments in Wesleyan Spirituality* (Kansas City: Beacon Hill Press of Kansas City, 1991), 128.

3. Greathouse, *Romans 1–8*, 179.

4. Lodahl, *Story of God*, 178.

5. Stuart Townend, "How Deep the Father's Love for Us." Copyright © 1995 Thankyou Music (PRS) (adm. worldwide at EMIC MGPublishing.com, excluding Europe, which is adm. by Kingswaysongs). All rights reserved. Used by permission.

6. John Wesley, *The Works of John Wesley*, 3rd ed. (London: Wesleyan Methodist Book Room, 1872; repr., Kansas City: Beacon Hill Press of Kansas City, 1986), 10:191.

7. Ibid., 188.

8. Townend, "How Deep the Father's Love."

Chapter 3

1. The pastor in this true story is the author, and the man being baptized is the author's son, Steve Spruce. The events recounted occurred on April 12, 2009, Easter Sunday, at Springfield, Illinois, First Church of the Nazarene.

2. William H. Willimon, *Word, Water, Wine, and Bread: How Worship Has Changed over the Years* (Valley Forge, PA: Judson Press, 1980), 27.

3. Martin, *Worship in the Early Church*, 105.

Chapter 4

1. *Wikipedia*, s.v. "United Methodist Church," http://en.wikipedia.org/wiki/United_Methodist_Church.

2. The United Methodist Church, "Baptism Is Forever," quoted from Mark Trotter, *A United Methodist Understanding of Baptism* (Nashville: Abingdon Press, 2001), UMC.org, http://www.umc.org/site/c.lwL4KnN1LtH/b.1697379/k.9027/Baptism_Overview.htm.

3. The Wesleyan Church, "The Sacraments: Baptism and the Lord's Supper," Articles of Religion, art. 17, Wesleyan.org, http://www.wesleyan.org/beliefs#part17.

4. Dennis Bratcher, ed., "The Holy Sacraments," The Articles of Religion (Free Methodist), art. 16, CRI/Voice, Institute, http://www.crivoice.org/creedfm.html.

5. The Churches of Christ in Christian Union, "What We Teach," http://www.cccuhq.org/explore/who-we-are/what-we-teach.

6. Essex Alliance Church, "Baptism," http://www.essexalliance.org/pages/page.asp?page_id=44881.

7. Church of God (Anderson, Indiana), "Do you believe persons have to be baptized in the Church of God in order to go to heaven?" quoted from Oral and Laura Withrow, *Meet Us at the Cross* (Anderson, IN: Warner Press, 1999), 25-31, Church of God Ministries, http://www.chog.org/do-you-believe-persons-have-be-baptized-church-god-order-go-heaven.

8. Church of God (Anderson, Indiana), "Our History," Church of God Ministries, http://www.chog.org/our-history.

9. Assemblies of God USA, "Infant Baptism, Age of Accountability, Dedication of Children," General Council of the Assemblies of God, http://www.ag.org/top/beliefs/gendoct_11_accountability.cfm.

10. BBC, "Salvation Army," last updated July 30, 2009, http://www.bbc.co.uk/religion/religions/christianity/subdivisions/salvationarmy_1.shtml.

11. *Manual/2009-2013: Church of the Nazarene* (Kansas City: Nazarene Publishing House, 2009), par. 16.

12. Wesley, *Works of John Wesley*, 5:187.

13. Ibid., 189.

14. Staples, *Outward Sign and Inward Grace*, 98.

15. Wesley, *Works of John Wesley*, 5:189.

16. H. Ray Dunning, *Grace, Faith, and Holiness: A Wesleyan Systematic Theology* (Kansas City: Beacon Hill Press of Kansas City, 1988), 541.

17. Staples, *Outward Sign and Inward Grace*, 23.

Chapter 5

1. Author unknown.

2. Based on author's personal story.

3. Thomas à Kempis, *The Imitation of Christ* (New York: Hurst and Company, 1843), 123.

4. *Manual/2009-2013*, par. 800.1.

5. Willimon, *Word, Water, Wine, and Bread*, 30.

6. Ibid., 33.

Chapter 6

1. Author's personal story.

2. David Young (pastor of Clinton, Illlinois, Church of the Nazarene), comment offered while reviewing early draft of this book.

3. Joseph H. Mayfield, "John," in *John, Acts*, Beacon Bible Commentary, vol. 7 (Kansas City: Beacon Hill Press, 1965), 55.

4. John Wesley, *Letters of the Reverend John Wesley*, ed. John Telford (London: Epworth Press, 1931), 3:36.

5. Martin, *Worship in the Early Church*, 101.

6. Wesley, *Works of John Wesley*, 10:188.

7. Ibid., 189.

8. Ibid., 190.

9. Ibid.

10. *Manual/2009-2013*, par. 16.

11. J. Kenneth Grider, "Baptism," in *Beacon Dictionary of Theology*, ed. Richard S. Taylor (Kansas City: Beacon Hill Press of Kansas City, 1983), 64.

12. Alan Richardson, *An Introduction to the Theology of the New Testament* (New York: Harper and Row, 1958), 339.

13. George Allen Turner, "Infant Baptism (Con)," in *Beacon Dictionary of Theology*, 281.

14. J. Kenneth Grider, "Infant Baptism (Pro)," in *Beacon Dictionary of Theology*, 280.

15. *Manual/2009-2013*, pars. 16, 800.2, 800.3, 800.4.

16. Staples, *Outward Sign and Inward Grace*, 199-200.

17. *Manual/2009-2013*, par. 800.2.

18. Here a distinction could be made, according to Rob Staples, between children who were baptized as infants and those who were dedicated. On reaching the age of accountability, the emphasis for the former who are properly nurtured may be on making a personal confession of faith and owning their baptism. This would be highlighting the sacramental character of baptism, which points to what God has done through Christ for such persons and their inclusion in the body of Christ. The baptized, in essence, could potentially say a continual yes to God and thus maintain a saving relationship with Christ. However, for children dedicated as infants the emphasis would more likely be on confessing their sins and on having a personal conversion experience. In this case, the human intention and testimony of the parents is the focus. (See *Outward Sign and Inward Grace*, 192-95, 199-200.)

19. Dunning, *Grace, Faith, and Holiness*, 550.

20. Ibid.

21. Ibid., 550n38.

Chapter 7

1. The act of Christ's death that makes possible our salvation and reconciles us to God.

2. *Manual/2009-2013*, par. 6. (This wording contains amended language adopted by the 2009 General Assembly and ratified by district assemblies.)

3. Wesley, *Works of John Wesley*, 10:193.

4. Dunning, *Grace, Faith, and Holiness*, 550.

5. Jesse C. Middendorf, *The Church Rituals Handbook,* 2nd ed. (Kansas City: Beacon Hill Press of Kansas City, 2009), 28.

6. Wesley, *Works of John Wesley,* 10:508.